Finding Out About
INDUSTRIAL BRITAIN

Madeline Jones

Batsford Academic and Educational   *London*

Contents

Frontispiece:
An early industrial scene: the second bridge in Britain to be made from iron crosses the river Wear at Sunderland. On the right are furnaces for making glass.

Typeset by Tek-Art Ltd, Kent
and printed in Spain by
Grijelmo SA, Bilbao
for the publishers
Batsford Academic and Educational,
an imprint of B. T. Batsford Ltd,
4 Fitzhardinge Street
London W1H 0AH

ISBN 0 7134 4353 7

ACKNOWLEDGMENTS

Special thanks are due to Francis Celoria, Director of the Gladstone Pottery Museum, Sheila McGregor, Keeper of Fine Art, Atkinson Art Gallery, Southport, and Ian Taylor, Director of Big Pit Mining Museum.

The Author and Publishers thank the following for their permission to reproduce the illustrations: Big Pit Mining Museum, page 25; Central Electricity Generating Board, page 4; John Cornwell, page 12 (bottom); Gladstone Pottery Museum, pages 17, 41; The Medici Society Ltd, page 27; Michael Rawcliffe, page 12 (top); Science Museum, London, page 8; Richard Tames, page 11; Wales Tourist Board, page 21. The map on page 46 was drawn by Rudolph Britto.

Cover pictures The colour picture on the front cover shows the relocated old mine and colliery wagons at the open-air museum at Beamish (photograph by Bill Charlton). The left-hand picture shows Placing the kiln, c. 1845 (Gladstone Pottery Museum).

Introduction

Britain was the first country in the world to develop modern large-scale industries using complex machinery. This industrialization began about 200 years ago. Of course, there were industries in Britain long before that, but this book concentrates chiefly on the late eighteenth and the nineteenth centuries, when the big changes took place. In 1801, when the first census was taken, Britain was still largely rural, a country of nearly 11 million people, many of whom worked in agriculture. (The figures are all for Great Britain, that is England, Scotland and Wales, and do not include Ireland.) Towns, except for London with its 900,000 or so inhabitants, were small. By 1851, there were nearly 21 million people, London had a population of over 2 million and seven other towns (Manchester, Sheffield, Birmingham, Bradford, Bristol, Leeds and Liverpool) had populations of over 100,000. By 1881, two out of three British people lived in urban areas. By 1901, Britain's population was close to 37 million, and far more worked in industry than on the land.

For some, these changes were exciting and to be welcomed. Thomas Telford, one of Britain's great engineers, wrote to a friend in 1799:

We are making rapid progress in this country – I mean from Liverpool to Bristol, and from Wales to Birmingham. This is an extensive and rich district, abounding in coal, lime, iron and lead. Agriculture too is improving and manufactures are advancing at rapid strides towards perfection. Think of such a mass of population, industrious, intelligent and energetic, in continual exertion.

For others, this "Industrial Revolution" meant hardship or ruin. The fate of one group of skilled hand-workers, the "croppers", who trimmed the surface of woollen cloth with heavy shears, was described by William Dodd in his book *The Factory System Illustrated* (1841):

In 1814, there were 1,733 croppers in Leeds, all in full employment; and now, since the introduction of machinery the whole of the cloth . . . is dressed by a comparatively small number, chiefly boys, at from 5s to 8s [a week] . . . . The old croppers have turned themselves to any thing they can get to do; some acting as bailiffs, water-carriers, scavengers, or selling oranges, cakes, tapes and laces, gingerbread . . .

Moreover, though Britain had the great advantage of being the first modern industrial country and did not face serious competition until the 1870s, there were periods of slump (or recession) when trade was bad, firms went bankrupt and workers lost their jobs. Even when trade was good, working conditions in some industries were dreadful, especially in the early days of industrialization.

You can see why there are many arguments between historians who study Industrial Britain over the advantages and disadvantages of industrialization. Did the lives of ordinary people get better or worse? How long did it take for more than a few rich people to benefit from industrial growth? What did employers and governments do to try to help the people who suffered from the changes? What could people do to help themselves? You will find yourself trying to answer some of these questions as you read this book.

Samuel Smiles, a Victorian who praised (and wrote a book about) "Self Help", put forward one view in 1863. He was concerned about the suffering but felt that, in the end, modern

Britain produces very advanced machines today, like this underwater "Robot", which is designed to dig trenches under the Channel to carry electric power cables to France. The name of the firm which designed and developed the machine is on its side. Rigging International of Middlesbrough actually built it.

industry meant a better life for everybody. In the conclusion to his book, *Industrial Biography*, he wrote:

> In early times the products of skilled industry were for the most part luxuries intended for the few, whereas now the most exquisite tools and engines are employed in producing articles of ordinary consumption for the great mass of the community. Machines with millions of fingers work for millions of purchasers – for the poor as well as the rich.

Today, tours are organized to old industrial areas. ▷
Jokes were made when Bradford (famous for woollen goods) first advertised itself as a holiday centre. Bradford has had the last laugh, though: 10,000 package holidays there have been sold, and in 1983 Bradford won an award from the English Tourist Board.

Useful Sources

There is a great mass of material of all kinds to help us find out about Industrial Britain. This short book can only give you a small sample: you will be able to discover more for yourselves.

1. PEOPLE TO ASK

a) *The Librarian* of the reference or local history section of your public library will be able to suggest books about the Industrial Archaeology of your area (that is, about old industrial buildings, transport systems, mines, quarries, etc) as well as telling you what maps or pictures the library has.

b) *Older friends or relations* may have information to give about their own experiences in industry.

2. THE LOCAL AREA

Look around you: are there any old industrial buildings in your area? Is there a Victorian railway station or a canal? Do local street names tell you anything about the industrial past – names like Brick Lane or Furnace Hill? Even your own town or village may have a name connected with some local industry or industrialist like Port Sunlight (called after Sunlight Soap) or Wattstown in the Rhondda Valley, Wales. Perhaps your town has produced its own Town Trail, showing old industrial landmarks.

3. VISUAL MATERIAL

a) *Maps and illustrations* Ask at your library for old maps, especially large-scale Ordnance Survey maps (like the 6" to the mile, and the 25") produced in the nineteenth century. You can track down old industries on these, and compare them with a modern map. Ask if the library, or your local museum, has any old photographs or early prints or paintings of your area.

b) *Machinery* You can see machines, some of them actually working, in many museums. Look at pages 45-46 for a list.

4. WRITTEN SOURCES

a) *Local histories and industrial histories* Histories of counties and towns and of various industries written in the eighteenth or nineteenth centuries can give valuable information. They are often well-illustrated too.

b) *Guides and directories* Old guidebooks can tell you much about the history of your area. In nineteenth-century town directories, you can find details about local industries and sometimes lists of people living in every street, giving their occupations.

c) *Newspapers* Ask in your reference library if they have back-copies of local newspapers. You may find reports of factories or mines opening and closing, advertisements for jobs in local industries, reports of disasters or of strikes. Look at the goods advertised for sale too, and at the means of travel in your area at different periods.

d) *Diaries or memoirs* Sometimes industrialists (or their wives) kept diaries or wrote about their industries. A few working-people also managed to write diaries or autobiographies. You will find some examples in this book.

e) *Census material* Your reference library may have copies of the original answers to Victorian census questions. These are called the Census Returns, and are especially useful from 1851 on, as they then give occupation and place of birth for everyone in the area. (Because they give so much private information, they are not opened to the public for 100 years, so at present you cannot see any later than 1881.) Pick a street near an old factory

This advertisement comes from a guidebook of 1886. What important improvement for the home does it show? What does it tell you about a firm which still exists today? Do you know what Doulton is now famous for producing?

in your town, or near the gas works, and see what you can find out about the people who lived there a hundred or more years ago.

f) *Parliamentary papers* The many Reports of Parliamentary committees etc on industrial matters have all been printed. Large libraries may have copies of some of these. Many libraries will have collections of extracts from them, like those made by E. Royston Pike (see page 47). Your library may also have back-copies of *Hansard*, which records all parliamentary debates.

Coal and Iron

Britain was lucky in having plenty of coal and iron-ore. Early in the eighteenth century, Abraham Darby started to use coke (made from coal) instead of charcoal (made from scarce wood) to smelt iron at his ironworks at Coalbrookdale in Shropshire. Iron could now be produced more efficiently and cheaply, especially by ironworks on or near coalfields. More and more things, large and small, were made from it.

IRON NEEDED FOR LANCASHIRE'S INDUSTRIES, 1795

A considerable iron foundry is established in Salford, in which are cast most of the articles wanted in Manchester and its neighbourhood, consisting chiefly of large cast wheels for the cotton machines; cylinders, boilers, and pipes for steam engines . . .
(Aikin, *A Description of Manchester, 1795*)

Which new inventions have increased the demand for iron by the end of the eighteenth century?

"BLACK SHEFFIELD"

In spite of the surrounding ugliness, an iron-works in action was a spectacular sight. Travellers like William Cobbett in 1830 were impressed:

All the way along from Leeds to Sheffield it is coal and iron, and iron and coal. It was dark before we reached Sheffield, so that we saw the iron furnaces in all the horrible splendour of their everlasting blaze. Nothing can be conceived more grand or more terrific than the yellow waves of fire that incessantly issue from the top of these furnaces, some of which are close by the way-side. Nature has placed the beds of iron and the beds of coal alongside of each other, and art has taught man to make one to operate upon the other, as to turn the iron-stone into liquid matter, which is drained off from the bottom of the furnace, and afterwards moulded into blocks and bars, and all sorts of things. The combustibles [*things to be burnt*] are put into the top of the furnace, which stands thirty, forty or fifty feet up in the air, and the ever-blazing mouth of which is kept supplied with coal and coke and iron-stone from little iron waggons forced up by steam, and brought down again to be refilled. It is a surprising thing to behold, and it is impossible to behold it without being convinced that . . . other nations . . . will never equal England with regard to things made of iron and steel. This Sheffield, and the land all about it, is one bed of iron and coal. They call it black Sheffield, and black enough it is, but from this one town and its environs [*neighbourhood*] go nine-tenths of the knives that are used in the whole world . . .

Notice what type of power is being used to move waggons in these ironworks of 1830.

What comment could you make about Cobbett's statement that "other nations . . . will never equal England with regard to things made of iron and steel"?

IRON FROM SOUTH WALES IN USE IN SWITZERLAND

Britain first began to export iron in 1797. In 1838, Lady Charlotte Guest, wife of the owner of Dowlais Ironworks, was pleased to spot the firm's products when she and her husband visited a foundry at Zurich:

> **The man who went round with us did not know where the Bar Iron came from, but in poking about in the forge I found two or three bars upon which was the mark '*G.L. best*' (standing for Guest, Lewis & Co.) which settled the question very satisfactorily. It gave me for a moment as much pleasure to find my own Iron in this remote spot as anything has done during the journey . . .** (*Diary of Lady Charlotte Guest*)

John Guest's firm also made rails for the Russian railways.

A SHEFFIELD FIRM ADVERTISES ITS PRODUCTS, 1822

As well as machines and large structures like bridges or pit winding-gear, many smaller articles were made from iron. You'll find some of them listed in the following advertisement:

> **Green & Pickslay, manufacturers of the patent economical kitchen range, gas light apparatus makers and fitters up to the Gas Light Company, 14, High Street, ironmongers, cutlers, silversmiths, bell hangers, braziers, lockmakers, whitesmiths, ironfounders, hinge-makers, fenders and stove grate manufacturers. George's Street.** (*Directory of Sheffield, 1822*)

What iron goods are this firm making for the home?

Gas (made from coal) was used to light Sheffield streets from 1819. What work did this new invention bring to firms like Green & Pickslay?

By the end of the nineteenth century, colliery winding machinery (which lowered miners down the pit) was made of iron, and the ropes were of steel. This "Pit-head frame . . . elegant in appearance and of great strength, as made by Messrs Thornewill & Warham, engineers, of Burton-on-Trent, and erected at the Earl of Carnarvon's New Hall Park Collieries, near Burton-on-Trent" was 40 feet high. It was the type thought safest and recommended by The Colliery Manager's Handbook published in 1891.

Can you find anything else made of iron in this picture?

Machines and Factories

The "machine age" really began in eighteenth-century Britain when Richard Arkwright and Samuel Crompton made power-driven machines to spin cotton. From then on, more and more machines were invented to do work previously done by hand. Large machines were set up in "mills" or "manufactories", though at first these were few in number, and most workers continued to work at home or in small workshops. A factory often employed hundreds of workers who had to obey strict rules. Machines brought benefits – more and cheaper goods, help with heavy physical work, and new jobs *making* machines and their spare parts. Handworkers who lost their jobs suffered, however, and some attacked factories and destroyed machines. You might like to find out for yourselves about the "Luddites" who acted in this way.

You can see this example of Arkwright's water-powered spinning machine – the "water-frame" – in the Science Museum in London. What material is this early machine mostly made from? (You'll find a clue to this in Arkwright's advertisement for workmen.)

ARKWRIGHT ADVERTISES FOR WORKERS

In 1771, Richard Arkwright decided to set up his spinning machines in Cromford, Derbyshire. He put this advertisement in the *Derby Mercury*:

> **Cotton Mill, Cromford,
> 10 December 1771**
> **WANTED immediately, two
> Journeymen Clock-makers, or others
> that understands Tooth and Pinion
> well: Also a Smith that can forge and
> file – likewise two Wood Turners that
> has been accustomed to Wheelmaking,
> Spoke turning etc. Weavers residing at
> the Mill may have good Work. There is
> Employment at the above Place for
> Women, Children, etc. and good Wages.**

If you look at the picture you'll see why Arkwright needed clockmakers as well as other craftsmen to make his machines.

Notice that the jobs at the mill were mainly for women and children (though Arkwright hoped that whole families would settle in Crompton, with the men working at home as hand-loom weavers).

A HARD ROUTINE

Unlike those working at home, factory workers or "mill-hands" had no control over their daily timetable.

> **Rising at or before day-break, between
> four and five o'clock . . . [the factory
> worker] swallows a hasty meal, or
> hurries to the mill without taking any
> food whatever. At eight o'clock half an
> hour, and in some instances forty
> minutes, are allowed for breakfast. In
> many cases, the engine continues at
> work during mealtime, obliging the
> labourer to eat and still overlook his**

MACHINES REPLACE WORKERS

By the 1820s some weaving was also being done by machines called power-looms. Hand-loom weavers were less in demand. A Committee of hand-loom weavers in Manchester wrote in 1823:

> **Power-looms by diminishing the demand for manual labour, have put the manual weaver entirely in the power of his Employer. The Employers can throw their Weavers out of Employ when they please, without injury to themselves. While thousands are glad of Employ at any wages whatever.**
> (Quoted by J.C. and Barbara Hammond, *The Town Labourer, 1760-1832,* published 1917)

As spinning-machines were further developed they needed fewer workers to operate them, and some employers found this very useful. In Manchester, during a strike of cotton-spinners in 1824,

> **the idea occurred to the masters that it might be possible to make the spinning-mules run out and in at the proper speed by means of self-acting machinery ... [A Mr. Roberts produced suitable machines – needing the labour only] of a few boys and girls to watch them and mend the broken threads ...**
> (Samuel Smiles, *Industrial Biography,* 1863)

What do you think happened to the striking cotton-spinners? Can you think of any modern examples of machines replacing workers? What can be done to help people who lose jobs because new machinery is developed?

> **work .... This meal is brought to the mill .... At twelve o'clock the engine stops, and an hour is given for dinner. The hands leave the mill, and seek their homes .... If, as often happens, the majority of the labourers reside at some distance, a great portion of the allotted time is necessarily taken up by the walk, or rather the run, backwards and forward .... Again they are closely immured [*shut in*] from one o'clock till eight or nine, with the exception of twenty minutes, this being allowed for tea .... During the whole of this long period they are actively and unremittingly engaged in a crowded room and elevated [*high*] temperature ...** (P. Gaskell, *The Manufacturing Population of England,* 1833)

Though the worker in this passage is referred to as "he", the whole family was likely to work at the mill.

Here you see the much more elaborate spinning machines of the early twentieth century. What material are they made from? What do you notice about the people working in this spinning-mill?

Power

Wind power and water power had been used for centuries before 1700 to grind corn, and water power had been used for other things, too – to move bellows in iron furnaces, for example. In the eighteenth century water power was also used for running textile machinery, first for silk-spinning and then for cotton-spinning machines like Arkwright's water-frame. A steam-powered engine (Newcomen's engine) was invented in 1709. It could only move a beam up and down, but was widely used to drain coal mines (which also provided the coal to heat water to make steam). Then in 1782, James Watt patented a steam engine which would make wheels go round and round (a rotative engine). More complicated steam-driven machines could now be developed. By the 1830s, steam engines were pulling railway trains, and steamships were crossing the Atlantic. Steam remained the main source of power for industry until, in the twentieth century, it was replaced by electricity.

SOURCES OF POWER FOR INDUSTRIES IN SHEFFIELD AND CARLISLE

The Yorkshire writer Edward Baines, whose father had once owned part of a cotton-spinning factory at Brindle which made use of an old water-powered corn-mill, lived to see many local industries make the change to steam.

> **The year 1742 is memorable in the history of this place [Sheffield] for the introduction of a new manufacture [silver plate] ... various companies were formed ... the streams and the falls of the Don and Sheaf furnished a powerful agent for rolling out the metal in mills erected for that purpose. ... In 1786, the first steam-engine grinding wheel was erected ... and the agency of water has since been in a great measure superseded in the large manufactories, by the use of that much more certain and efficient power – steam.** (Baines's *Yorkshire*, vol 1, 1822)

Why is steam generally more "certain" than water as a source of power? (What might happen in a hot summer?) You'll see from the Samuel Smiles extract, though, that early steam engines could be rather uncertain themselves!

Some factories continued to use water power well after the invention of steam engines:

> **The spinning of cotton by machinery ... has been carried on here [Carlisle] to a very considerable extent, and large quantities of cotton twist are now exported from the eleven cotton mills in Carlisle and its neighbourhood, which contain collectively about 80,000 spindles, put in motion by means of five waterwheels and six steam engines ...** (*History Directory and Gazetteer of Cumberland and Westmorland*, Parson & White, 1829)

Battersea Power Station has been a London landmark ▷ *since it opened in 1931. It used coal to provide electricity. In 1983, after it was closed down because it had become too old-fashioned, the public were allowed in to look round and a competition was launched to decide a future use for the splendid building with its large halls. Can you find out what ideas were put forward, or make a suggestion yourself?*

PROBLEMS WITH EARLY STEAM ENGINES

Samuel Smiles, writing in 1863, looked back to the early years of the steam engine:

> Not fifty years since it was a matter of the utmost difficulty to set an engine to work, and sometimes of equal difficulty to keep it going. Though fitted by competent workmen, it often would not go at all. Then the foreman of the factory at which it was made was sent for, and he would almost live beside the engine for a month or more; and after easing her here and screwing her up there, putting in a new part and altering an old one, packing the piston and tightening the valves, the machine would at length be got to work. Now the case is altogether different. The perfection of modern machine-tools is such that the utmost possible precision is secured . . .

Why did the improvements in machine tools (for making the various parts of engines) make such a difference?

STEAM POWER ALTERS THE LOCATION OF INDUSTRY

The Scottish journalist David Bremner explained in his 1869 account of *The Industries of Scotland* what a difference the invention of Watt's steam engine had made:

> It was no longer necessary for one proposing to build a mill to range the country in search of a waterfall of a sufficient strength to keep his machinery going, and, having found such – it might be far away from any centre of population – to convey thither not only the appliances and material necessary to carry on the work but to induce an adequate number of work people to take up their abode in the neighbourhood of the mill. The steam engine enabled him to set up his mill in the midst of the people.

What else did a factory using steam power need, as well as work people? (Think of how steam is produced.) Where would it be most sensible to build such a factory?

Changing Landscapes

Industry brought dramatic changes to some areas. Mines and ironworks, with their mounds of waste and their workmen's cottages, spread across the countryside. Tall factory chimneys dominated growing towns. Local people often had to live with industrial pollution, but they needed the work that new industries provided.

Factory chimneys became local landmarks, like this one in Sheffield.

"EVERYTHING WAS CHANGED"

In 1860, John Ward, a weaver from Clitheroe who kept a diary, revisited the places he had known as a child.

1860 April 6, Good Friday.
... I thought I would go to Hyde and Newton Moor, where I had lived many years when I was a boy and young man.
... It was twenty-eight years since I was in that road before, but now everything was changed. Villages have grown into large towns, and country places where there was nothing but fields are now covered with streets, and villages and large factories and workshops everywhere.

A NEW INDUSTRIAL TOWN: MIDDLESBROUGH

In 1829 only 40 people lived in the area of Middlesbrough. By 1861, after a port for shipping coal and an iron industry had been developed there, 19,416 people lived in a growing town. By 1901, with steel now the main industry, there were 91,000 inhabitants. The Prince of Wales opened the new Town Hall in 1887 and made a joke about the town's smoke. The Mayor replied:

His Royal Highness owned he had expected to see a smoky town. It is one, and if there is one thing more than another that Middlesbrough can be said to be proud of, it is the smoke.... The smoke is an indication of plenty of work ... an indication of prosperous times ... an indication that all classes of workpeople are being employed, that there is little necessity for charity ... and that even those in the humblest station are in a position free from want. Therefore we are proud of our smoke.
(Quoted in Asa Briggs, *Victorian Cities*, (1963))

Why was the Mayor of Middlesbrough pleased to see his town filled with smoke? Why is there much less smoke from industry today? (You'll find part of the answer to this in the Date List (page 45) – look at the entry for 1956 – but you'll probably be able to think of other reasons too.)

Blaenavon in Gwent grew up around an iron-works, started in 1789, and a number of coal-pits. This pit produced coal from 1880 to 1980. It is now Big Pit Mining Museum. Beyond the buildings you can see the remains of the old waste-heaps – the "tips". Once these were much bigger. Mining areas were dominated by tips and by the pits' winding-gear, which you can spot at once in the picture.

CHANGE IN THE WELSH VALLEYS

William Thomas was born in the Rhondda Valley, South Wales, in 1843, before most of the mines there opened. He worked for a time as a miner himself, and expressed the mixed feelings of local people towards new industries in their areas:

I wish no harm to trade and industry; these things must be. I don't wish to say a word against those who are risking their money in seeking the coal and destroying the beauty of the countryside. I wish them all success, and success also to the brave men, the miners who venture into the earth's depths after the coal, but oh! in so doing they are defacing my beloved country ...
(*History of Llanwynno*, 1888)

Today, many mines have closed (only one colliery is left in the Rhondda, which once had over 50) and the landscape has changed again. If you go to Aberdare in South Wales, you can follow either an Industrial Trail or a Nature Trail through the Dare Valley Country Park, created from the old mining area.

A VICTORIAN GUIDE-BOOK DESCRIBES A POLLUTED LANDSCAPE

The copper-works and other manufactories are situated along the sides of the river, at about a mile and a half from the town [Swansea]; and here the atmosphere is beclouded and vitiated [*made unpleasant*] by the fumes of copper, sulphur, arsenic, etc., and the face of the country, deprived of its verdure [*greenery*], is rendered barren and unsightly. (*Black's Picturesque Guide to South Wales*, 1886)

Why would this area have been unpleasant to live in?

The New Masters

Men who built up new industries worked hard. They liked to live near their factory or works. Some of them took a fatherly interest in their work-people. Others were remembered for their harshness like Joseph Bailey and his brother, who owned Nantyglo Ironworks in Gwent. (They had to build round towers to protect themselves from possible attacks from their workers in the 1830s.)

IRONMASTERS' HOUSES IN SOUTH WALES OVERLOOK THE IRONWORKS

[Mr. Crawshay's house at Merthyr] is surrounded with fire, flame, smoke, and ashes. The noise of hammers, rolling mills, forges and bellows, incessantly din and crash upon the ear. Bars and pigs of iron are continually thrown to the hugely accumulating heaps that threaten to choke up every avenue of access [*way into the house*]. (B.H. Malkin, *The Scenery, Antiquities and Biography of South Wales*, 1804)

This house, Soho House, was built in 1762 by Matthew Boulton near his new works at Soho, just outside Birmingham.

Lady Charlotte Guest was taken as a young bride to her husband's house near his ironworks at Dowlais:

By the time we reached the house it was quite dark and the prevailing gloom gave full effect to the light of the blazing furnaces, which was quite unlike all I had ever before seen or even imagined . . . we walked out as far as the limits of the garden, round the house, and stood without [*outside*] the gate – "the furnace gate" – upon the steps leading to the works . . . (Lady Charlotte Guest, *Diary*, 15 August 1833)

Later, John Guest bought a country estate in Dorset and the family moved there. Even if the founder of a business stayed in his nearby house, his sons usually moved away. Why, do you think? Try making up a family discussion about whether or not to move: remember to point out the advantages as well as the disadvantages of living on the spot.

Thomas Ashton and his brothers owned several textile factories at Hyde near Manchester. Conditions of work there were good, and Ashton took a great interest in the houses the firm built and rented to its workers. These had one unusual feature for workers' houses at this time. Ashton was questioned about this by the Commission on the State of Large Towns in 1844:

Thomas Ashton Esq. examined

Are you a manufacturer at Hyde, near Manchester?

Yes.

How many labourers' houses have you there?

About 320.

Have you introduced water into these houses?

Yes, into every house. I was at the expense of putting down the tenants' communication pipe [*joining the house to the Water Main*]; the total cost was about £1 [per house]. I charge them 1s per annum for this tap, which is included in the rent of the water, which is 3d per week, and is charged by me for this convenience. I pay it quarterly to the water company.

Has the change . . . given satisfaction to your tenants?

Very great indeed . . . there is never any complaint in paying for the water . . .

You say you have introduced the water into every house; do you mean even the most humble habitation?

Yes . . .

Notice that Ashton does not give the water free of charge (how long will it take him to cover the cost of putting the water-pipes into the houses?)

The younger generation could sometimes be awkward about following in father's footsteps. The next extract comes from *Danesbury House*, a story by a famous Victorian writer, Mrs Henry Wood. Her hero, Arthur Danesbury, was the eldest son of the owner of an ironworks.

Arthur was now in partnership with his father, receiving a small share of the profits. . . . William [the next brother] was in London, articled to an eminent firm . . . [of] Civil Engineers. His future destination was likewise to be the Danesbury Works, where he would take the head of the engineering department.

The younger children, Robert and Lionel, had left school this midsummer . . .

"Now that it is decided you do not go to school again" [said their father] "you must choose what you will be. I should prefer you both coming to the works; there is room for all of you . . ." Robert Danesbury turned up his nose. The two boys had been to a noted aristocratic private school, where they had learnt thoroughly to despise 'business'. . .

(In the book, Robert insisted on joining the Army – and he came to a bad end.) Mrs Henry Wood suggests one reason why sons might not want to follow their fathers into industry (Victorian daughters were not given the chance). Can you think of any other possible reasons? Would you say there was any prejudice against a career in industry today? Or not?

The Workers

New industries meant new opportunities for some working people. So did building projects and the new methods of transport (see pages 30-31). Even in the second half of the nineteenth century, though, many industrial workers continued to work in small workshops or in their own homes.

LEAVING THE LAND

Alexander Somerville, born 1811, was a farm-labourer's son. He looked back without regret on his childhood home in Coldingham, on the east coast of Scotland, a single-roomed house where his father and mother lived with their eight children:

> The place [was] without ceiling or anything beneath the bare tiles of the roof; without a floor save the common clay; without a cupboard or recess of any kind; with no grate but the iron bars which the tenants carried to it, built up and took away when they left it; with no partition of any kind save what the beds made ... (Alexander Somerville, *Autobiography of a Working Man*, 1848)

NEW SKILLS NEEDED

New industries found it difficult to get the right kind of workers. Samuel Smiles, the Victorian author, described the problems faced by late eighteenth-century pioneers like James Watt and his partner, Matthew Boulton:

> For a long time we find Watt in his letters complaining to his partner of the failure of his engines through 'villainous bad workmanship'. Sometimes the cylinders, when cast, were found to be more than an eighth of an inch wider at one end than the other, and under such circumstances it was impossible the engine could act with precision. Yet better work could not be had. First-rate workmen in machinery did not as yet exist; they were only in process of education. (S. Smiles, *Lives of the Engineers,* vol IV, 1878)

Look at the next section *Wages* (pages 18-19) and you'll find an example of a young man who had the right skill to do well in early nineteenth-century industry.

What new skills are needed by workers in today's most modern industries?

MOVING AWAY TO WORK

Not surprisingly, Alexander Somerville left farm work: in 1830 he was earning 11s. per week working as a labourer on a new harbour being built near Coldingham.

> We had stone-masons at the Cove who had come from Edinburgh, Glasgow, Dundee, Berwick and Newcastle, some of whom were literally without a shirt, and without tools when they came; who borrowed tools, borrowed shirts, earned 18s. a week and drank it all in whisky, week after week, for months together ...

Notice that the stone-masons, skilled men, earn more than the young labourers. What do you think all these workers would do when the harbour was finished?

WORKING AT HOME

It was a long time before most industries completely changed over to a factory system. In the Black Country (around Wolverhampton) nail-making was an old-established craft. In the 1860s, an American living in England found many nail-makers still with their own small workshops (though he commented that he thought they would soon find that machine-made nails would replace hand-made ones).

> **We called in at one [at Halesowen] . . . and had a long talk with the woman at her anvil. She was the head of the establishment, and a cheery, pleasant-spoken mother of four children. . . . Her husband was a collier, and she alone carried on the nail-making. . . . She could only be four days of the week at the forge, because, as she said, she had to 'fettle' about the house, washing and mending for the family and doing other wife's work. . . . She could only earn between three and four shillings a week at the anvil; but that was a great help to them, and helped out her husband's wages.** (Elihu Burritt, *Walks in the Black Country*, 1868)

Can you find anything in this passage that tells you about Victorian attitudes to women? Why was the collier's wife willing to do this work though it brought in so little money? Do you know of any modern examples of women working at home for very low pay?

Work in the Potteries was more varied than factory work, but it was also heavy. Here men are loading the kiln with "saggers" – clay boxes filled with dishes to be baked hard. Can you see how the saggers are arranged in a space-saving way? How are the men carrying their loads?

Wages

In the nineteenth century, wages varied from industry to industry and from place to place and even from worker to worker (at Huntley & Palmer's biscuit factory in Reading, workers of the same sex doing the same job were not all paid the same wage until 1914). Skilled men and women could do well, and even the unskilled were generally better paid in industry than on the land. There was no security, though – a slump in demand for goods brought wage-cuts or unemployment.

WAGES IN TEXTILE FACTORIES IN ASHTON-UNDER-LYNE, 1844

... the labouring classes of the town are nearly all employed in cotton-spinning ... and in calico manufacturing by means of power-looms ... the following wages per week can usually be realized [*gained*] by factory operatives when the mills are running full time, viz. dressers 27s, over-lookers 26s, engineers 25s, spinners 22s 6d, warehouse men 15s, twisters-in 14s, weavers 10s, card-room hands 9s, winders 8s 6d, warpers 8s 6d, reelers 8s 6d, big piecers 8s 6d, and little piecers 4s 6d. (*Report of Commission on State of Large Towns, 1844*)

What do you think "big piecers" and "little piecers" were? Notice the remark "when the mills are running full time": what would happen to wages when they weren't?

A SKILLED WORKER RISES IN THE WORLD

James Beaumont Neilson, a Scot born in 1792, was able to improve his financial position. Notice, though, that even his career had its ups and downs:

[Beaumont came from a colliery engine-worker's family and first worked for his brother] at a guinea a week, after which, in 1814 ... he was appointed engine-wright of [a] colliery at a salary of from £70 to £80 a year ... his master ... becoming unfortunate in business, he was suddenly thrown out of employment.... About this time a gas-works, the first in Glasgow, was projected ... the directors advertised for a superintendent and foreman, to whom they offered a 'liberal salary'... [Beaumont] was one of twenty candidates, and the fortunate one; and in August 1817 we find him appointed foreman of the Glasgow Gasworks, at a salary of £90 a year ... he was reappointed for six years more, at the advanced salary of £200, with the status of manager and engineer of the works. His salary was gradually increased to £400 a year, with a free dwelling-house ... (Samuel Smiles, *Industrial Biography*, 1863)

Which new industry gave Neilson his big chance? What was looked on as "a liberal salary" for a foreman in 1817?

WHAT WAGES COULD BUY

Because money-values have changed so much, you need to find out something about what money would buy in the nineteenth century. For example, the 1844 Report on Ashton goes on to tell us that the weekly rent of a good 4-roomed cottage was 3/6 per week and of a 2-roomed cottage, 2s per week. Here is an account of the meals provided by a Derbyshire foundry-worker's wage in 1855. As a skilled man, he earned 27s 8d a week. He had a wife and four children and spent 14s a week on food (he also had a garden – why is it important to know that?)

> Breakfast at 7   Parents – tea or coffee, with milk and sugar. Bread and butter and cold meat.   Children – bread and milk.
> Dinner at noon.   Meat, bread, potatoes, vegetables: fruit or cheese.
> Tea at 4.   Tea, sugar, bread and butter.
> Supper at 8.   Remains of dinner.
> (Material collected by Le Play, 1855, and quoted by John Burnett, *Plenty and Want*, 1966)

A TEEN-AGE GIRL AND HER WAGES

Women were paid less than men in most industries. However, Lancashire "mill girls" could earn higher wages than most women. Some were able to live well:

> Jane L., aged 18, born in Manchester of Irish parents . . . learned weaving and has been a power-loom weaver ever since. Has four looms, earns 13s. a week, and pays her 'little helper' 3s. a week besides, so her gross earnings are 16s. Gives her mother 7s. a week and keeps the rest of her wages herself . . .

GETTING YOUR WAGES PAID

Some unscrupulous employers would not pay all a worker's wage in cash. Instead, vouchers for the company-shop were given (what kind of prices could company-shops charge if workers *had* to get their goods there?) Laws were passed against these "truck" or "tommy" shops, but they were not obeyed. A character in Benjamin Disraeli's novel *Sybil* (1845) explains why workers could not insist on their rights:

> 'But he [the owner's agent] cannot force you to take goods', said the stranger; 'he must pay you in current coin of the realm, if you demand it'. 'They only pay us once in five weeks', said a collier; 'and how is a man to live meanwhile? And suppose we were to make shift [*manage*] for a month or five weeks, and have all our money coming and have no tommy out of the shop, what would the butty [*the mine-owner's agent*] say to me? He would say, 'Do you want . . . a note [*a voucher for the tommy-shop*] this time? and if I was to say 'No', then he would say 'You've no call to go down to work any more here. . . .'

> The [silk] gown she has on cost her £1.16.6d., her bonnet cost £1.9s. She wears silk gloves, they cost her about 1s. 6d. per pair. Shoes cost her about 15s. a year . . . (*Factory Commission, 1st Report, 1833*)

On what does Jane seem to spend most of her money? Notice the wage she pays the child who works with her: and notice that her parents are immigrants to Manchester. Where have they come from? Why do you think they moved to Manchester?

Working Conditions

In the nineteenth century, and especially in the early days of new industries, working conditions were often very bad. Reformers concentrated at first on the state of the child-workers, and the first Factory Acts and the 1842 Mines Act tried to improve things for them (you'll find information about these Acts on pages 44-45).

FACTORY CHILDREN

It was difficult to keep young children awake for the long hours they had to work in the early factories. This is what one "overlooker" (supervisor) in a flax-mill told a committee set up by the House of Commons in 1832 to investigate conditions of child-workers in factories. He was asked:

> **Do you think you could have got the quantity of work out of the children for so great a number of hours [6 a.m.– 7 p.m., or 5 a.m.– 9 p.m. when the mill was busy] without . . . cruel treatment?**
> **– For that number of hours, I could not, I think; it is a long time. The speed of the machinery is calculated, and they [the masters] know how much work it will do; and unless they [the children] are driven and flogged up, they cannot get the quantity of work they want from them . . .**

The evidence collected by committees like this one provides good material for a play or recorded documentary. You'll find more examples in books listed on pages 46-47, especially those by E. Royston Pike. (You can find out, too, about wise employers like Robert Owen who treated their child workers well.)

WORKING IN THE POTTERIES

Men who worked in the Staffordshire Potteries were paid piece-rates (that is, according to the number of "pieces" of earthenware, china, etc, they produced in a week). This meant that they could choose how many hours to work each day. The men liked this, but it was hard on their helpers, as one boy later remembered:

> **I have said there was generally little, if any work, done on Mondays and Tuesdays, and yet it was rare for any of the men to get on Saturday less than a full week's wage. From Wednesday to Saturday they worked themselves, and worked others, boys and women, like galley slaves. From four and five in the morning until nine and ten at night this fierce race for wages was run. There was no Factory Act then, nor for a quarter of a century afterwards . . .**
> (C. Shaw (An Old Potter), *When I was a Child*, 1903)

The Factory Act of 1847 fixed a 10-hour day for all workers under 18 in textile factories, and this was extended to other industries in the 1860s.

It is still a very interesting experience to visit a ▷ coalmine and get some idea of miners' working conditions. These visitors are being shown round Big Pit Mining Museum, Blaenavon, by an ex-miner. What questions would you want to ask him? Notice the modern lamps on the helmets. You might like to find out for yourselves about earlier lamps, like the Davy Safety Lamp. Why is it unsafe to take a naked flame underground? (You'll find a clue to this in the next section.)

BRICKMAKING

As late as 1868 an American visitor to the "Black Country" (the area around Wolverhampton) found girls of around 13 doing heavy, unpleasant work in the brickmaking industry.

> A middle-aged woman ... her clothes ... bespattered and weighted with wet clay ... formed the clay dough into loaves ... with a dash, splash, and a blow one was perfectly shaped. One little girl then took it away.... Another girl, a little older, brought the clay to the bench. This was a heavier task.... She first took up a mass of the cold clay, weighing about twenty-five pounds, upon her head, and while balancing it there, she squatted to the heap without bending her body, and took up a mass of equal weight with both hands against her stomach and with the two burdens walked about a rod [*just over 5 metres*] and deposited them on the moulding bench ... (Elihu Burritt, *Walks in the Black Country*, 1868)

The girls were paid about 1s. each for a day's work of this kind.

A VISIT TO A COALMINE IN THE 1860s

Some workplaces were particularly dangerous and uncomfortable. (Coalmines still are, despite modern improvements: you'll find some evidence of this on pages 42-43.) When Scottish journalist David Bremner went down a mine he did not enjoy the experience.

> Our path – a main roadway be it recollected – was about four feet in width and barely so much in height. The bottom of it was laid with a line of rails, and the space between the rails was wet and muddy. Overhead, ugly rents yawned, and fragments of rock protruded in a most threatening way.... Progress was frequently interrupted by the passing of coal-laden hurleys, which were pushed along the rails by lads carrying lights on their foreheads, and an occasional pause was made to take advantage of some gaps in the roof, which permitted us to obtain some rest by standing erect ...
>
> [At the coal face they found miners working in a three-feet seam of coal.] The work ... is very hard and irksome – though we were told it was mere child's play when compared with the labour of excavating the 'low seams' the depth of which is only from twenty-two to twenty-four inches. In a three-feet seam, the miner can kneel while working; but in thin seams, he has to lie at length on his side, and in some cases water pours down on him continuously ... (*The Industries of Scotland*, 1869)

David Bremner went on to say that a miner's job was "a very perilous one". Read the next section and you'll see why.

Accidents

DANGEROUS MACHINERY

In the early factories, machinery was not fenced in or guarded as it is today. The first Factory Inspectors wanted laws passed to compel owners to make their machines safe to operate. Even the Inspectors themselves did not feel safe on their factory visits. T.J. Howell reported from the North West in April 1839:

> **There are various mills in my district . . . in which the machinery is so crowded and exposed as to be extremely dangerous; the law contains no provision authorising the inspector to interfere in this matter . . . but . . . I have experienced great personal hazard . . . the accidents which are perpetually occurring to the work-people in these places sufficiently indicate the danger.** (_Report of the Inspectors of Factories_, 1839)

It was not only textile machinery that was dangerous. The Commissioners investigating employment of children in 1843 were told about a Wolverhampton nail-making factory with a bad reputation for accidents.

> **Witness No.96, a boy aged 16 . . . works at Messrs. Hemingsley's nail and tip manufactory at Wolverhampton. Accidents happen there every week, very near; finger ends are continually pinched sometimes pinched off, or cut off . . .** (_Second Report of Children's Employment Commission, 1843_)

You can find out from the Date List (pages 44-45) when the first law was passed ordering machines to be guarded, and when workers gained the right to proper compensation for injury.

Many industries were dangerous to work in: some still are. After the 1833 Factory Act had provided Inspectors for Factories, and the 1850 Inspection of Coal Mines Act Inspectors for Mines, more attention was given to accident prevention. Even so, there were some sad incidents to report.

When an explosion occurred, or when men were trapped underground by a fall of rock, miners' wives and mothers waited at the pit-head for news. This scene was drawn for the Illustrated London News _in the 1890s, after a disaster at Parkslip Colliery. Why would the young woman in the front of the picture be especially badly off if her husband were dead?_

Explosions were not the only cause of mining accidents. What caused the greatest number of deaths in mines between 1851 and 1890?

(The table comes from The Colliery Manager's Handbook, _1891.)_

Deeper mines, needed to produce more coal for industry and steam transport, meant greater danger from exploding fire-damp (a mixture of air and methane gas that formed underground). A Commission "for preventing explosions in Coalmines" was investigating the subject in 1880, when yet another explosion occurred. Questions were asked in the House of Commons:

15 July 1880 *Sir R. Assheton Cross* (MP for Lancashire South West) asked the Secretary of State for the Home Department –
If he has received any information by telegraph . . . [about] the report which appears in the papers as to a terrible colliery explosion which has just taken place at Risca in South Wales . . .
Mr. Macdonald (MP for Stafford) also wished to ask . . .
Whether the loss of life is 118 or 128, and whether, considering the fact that previous explosions have occurred in the same vein of the same colliery – in 1846 when 14 lives were lost; in 1853 when 10 lives were lost, and in 1860, when 142 lives were lost – he will not at once send down a special commissioner to hold an enquiry . . . and ascertain whether the colliery regulations have been properly carried out?
Sir William Harcourt (Home Secretary) Sir, I have received this afternoon a telegram from Mr. Cadman, the local Inspector of Mines, in the following terms:–
'It is my painful duty to inform you that a firedamp explosion occurred at this [the Risca] colliery at 2 o'clock this morning. I believe 118 are killed. May I ask that Mr. Wales, of the adjoining district, may be telegraphed to assist me? Will wire you any further particulars again this evening'.
That is all the information I have yet received . . .
(*Hansard*, July 1880)

The Inspector of Mines gave the result of the Coroner's Inquest on the cause of death of the men killed at Risca in his 1880 Report:

120 persons were in the pit, all of whom lost their lives. . . . What caused the explosion the jury considered there was not evidence to prove, but they were all of the opinion that the colliery was well managed.

Why would the colliery authorities be relieved by this verdict? Do you think it would satisfy everybody?
Notice where the MPs first saw the news of what had happened at Risca – and also which "modern" invention was used to inform the Home Secretary. How do you think the news would reach these people today?

Number of deaths from explosions at collieries from 1851 to 1890. Inclusive.	Per cent. of the total.	Number of deaths from falls of roof and sides from 1851 to 1890. Inclusive.	Per cent. of the total.	Number of deaths from miscellaneous causes, above and below ground from 1851 to 1890. Inclusive.	Per cent. of the total.	Total number of deaths from all kinds of accidents from 1851 to 1890. Inclusive.
9,055	21·4	17,047	40·3	16,177	38·3	42,279
Averages per year } 226		426		405		1,057

Improvements

By the 1830s, people were becoming more aware of the hardships that many industrial workers endured. Facts and figures were produced by committees of MPs, Royal Commissions, individuals and local groups. Gradually, Parliament passed laws to shorten working hours and improve conditions in factories and mines. Industrial towns were improved, too, with better sanitation and housing. Employers aimed at higher standards in their factories. Trade Unions grew stronger and pressed for better working conditions as well as higher wages.

BETTER FACTORIES

The Scottish journalist David Bremner, writing in the 1860s, noticed how standards of factory-building had improved. Here he describes the new buildings at a jute factory (Camlerdown Works) near Dundee:

> The design of the buildings is characterised by much neatness; and an elegance and airiness pervade the place which show an extraordinary advance on the notions as to what a factory should be. It is not many years since the ideal of a factory was a hideously plain building of many low storeys, into which the light struggled through windows about two feet square, the dust and dirt on which it would have been considered something like sacrilege to have removed. Anything approaching to ventilation was not thought of, and, consequently, no provision was made for the admission of air to the sickly operatives. Now ... the storeys are from fourteen to seventeen feet in height, and every room is thoroughly ventilated.... It may be said that the Factory Acts are to some extent to be credited with this, but it is due to the owners of many of the factories to say that in the matters referred to they have far exceeded the requirements of the law.... The smoke from the furnaces is carried off by an ornamental chimney 300 feet in height and 35 feet in diameter at the base. The chimney alone cost over £3000....

Today, there are strict rules about ventilation, the number of people a room can hold, how hot or cold it can be, etc. If you want to find out about these, ask in your local reference library for a summary of the Health and Safety at Work Act of 1974. (There is a useful TUC *Guide* to the Act, first published in 1975.)

BETTER TIMES FOR CHILDREN

An elderly worker from the Potteries, writing in 1903, felt that he had seen conditions improve greatly since his own boyhood:

> Many a time, after fourteen and fifteen hours' work, I had to walk a mile and a half home with another weary little wretch.... Oh, yes, I have seen ghosts and heard their wailings on such nights, when my senses were dazed with weariness.... Boys don't see them now ... because the Factory Act sends them home at six o'clock, and because the road is lit up with gas lamps.
> (C. Shaw (An Old Potter), *When I was a Child*, 1903)

You'll notice that another improvement, as well as shorter hours is mentioned here: what is it?

House of Lords
Friday 16th July, 1880.
Viscount Middleton rose to call attention to the Report of the Royal Commission on Noxious Vapours [set up in 1876: Middleton was a member] and to ask Her Majesty's Government whether they proposed to introduce a measure in accordance with the recommendations contained in it? ... the Commission reported in 1878 [and a Bill, introduced in 1879, did not get passed before that Parliament ended]. ... Meanwhile, the evil went on in the manufacturing districts; and so bad became the air from the noxious vapours that even the telegraph wires became corroded ... experience had shown that where judicious pressure was put upon manufacturers science had responded to the touch, and a way had been found of remedying defects which had previously been declared to be impossible. ... He was perfectly aware that it was necessary to guard against over-legislation, lest trade might be driven abroad; but he believed that the recommendations of the Commissioners might be adopted without any danger of that ...
(*Hansard*, 1880)

Why did Viscount Middleton think that a law to prevent harmful smoke was needed? What problem was there about making too many regulations? Could these same arguments be put forward about any of today's pollution problems, do you think?

A great twentieth-century improvement for miners was the provision of pit-head baths (why was it so much better for the men if they could bath at work rather than at home?) These are the suggestions given to the miners using the baths at Big Pit, Blaenavon, which were opened in 1939: miners paid 6d per week from their wages to cover running costs.

What can you learn from the advice given here about working conditions underground at Big Pit? Why did each man need two lockers?

Going to Wash.

Entering the Baths by the pit entrance, clean your boots on the boot-cleaning apparatus (revolving brushes driven by electricity) so as to remove the dirt before entering the locker room.

On arriving at your pit clothes locker, undress and hang up your clothes in the locker.

EACH GARMENT MUST BE HUNG UP SEPARATELY AND SPREAD ROUND THE HOOKS AND THE DOOR OF THE LOCKER MUST BE SHUT. Each door is provided with a lock and key.

The clothes are dried by a current of warm air which is forced upwards through each locker. YOUR CLOTHES WILL NOT DRY:—

(1) If you bunch them together or throw them on the bottom of the locker. They will prevent the warm air from circulating and only the bottom garment will dry.

(2) If you hang up your singlet inside your shirt.

(3) If you leave the locker door open. The hot air will pass out through the door instead of circulating through the clothes.

(4) If the ventilation is not regulated properly by the attendants.

Pit boots may be slipped inside the rail near the bottom of the locker, the toe of the boot being tucked in in front of the rail; or the boots may be hung on one of the side hooks, or placed on the rack under the seat. **Don't stand them on the bottom of the locker** or they may get too dry and spoil.

Using your towel for a covering, take your soap-tray and go to the bath room through the opening marked with your Baths number. Use a cubicle marked with a coloured brick of the same colour as number plate on your locker. **Keep to these directions to avoid congestion, and to make the best use of the accommodation for all.**

There is a fitting in the cubicle to hold the soap-tray, and there are hooks at the cubicle entrance to hold your Towel, Locker Key and Shirt.

FINISH YOUR WASH WITH COLD WATER TO AVOID RISK OF CATCHING COLD.

After washing, take your towel and soap-tray and go through the nearest opening to your clean clothes locker. When dressed, leave your soap-tray and wet towel in your clean locker, where they will dry ready for your next shift.

The Attendant will supply towels and soap at prices fixed by the Management Committee, and posted up in the Baths.

In the lobby, where you leave the building, drinking fountains are provided.

Factory Inspectors

The reports of the Factory Inspectors tell us a great deal about factory conditions after 1833. At first, there were only four Inspectors with eight assistants. They were all men, and they only inspected textile factories. Gradually, their numbers increased (in 1983 there were 850), they were able to inspect all kinds of factories and workshops, and women Inspectors were appointed. You'll have noticed already (page 22) that the Factory Inspectors pressed for better safety measures in the factories, as well as seeing that the Factory Acts were obeyed. You have probably heard about the danger from asbestos dust. It was a Factory Inspector, Miss Whitlock, who first noticed how many breathing problems there were amongst workers in the asbestos factories she inspected in 1910.

TRYING TO ENFORCE THE 1833 FACTORY ACT

You can never safely assume that, because a reform is made into a law by Parliament, everyone at once obeys it. The 1833 Factory Act limited the number of hours worked by children under 13 to nine hours, and by 13-18 year olds to 12, and forbade children under 9 to work at all. Many attempts were made to dodge these regulations. In 1838, Mr Saunders, a Factory Inspector working in Yorkshire, found that mill-owners would choose certain doctors to give child workers their age certificates – doctors who

> 'will do the work better': which in general means some person who will certificate younger children as being 13 or 9 years of age . . .

Parents too tried to get round the rules:

> A parent will go to one surgeon [*doctor*] with his child, clean and in his best clothes, and if the surgeon does not think it 13, the parents immediately put on his working dress, higher shoes, and by the aid of the indigo [*dark-blue*] complexion obtained in a woollen mill, will endeavour to get a child a certificate of 13 from another surgeon...
>
> (*Reports of the Inspectors of Factories . . . December 1838*)

Why would the parents want the doctor to certify that their children were 13? How do we prove our ages today?

A SURPRISE VISIT TO A WOOLLEN-MILL AT OSSETT, YORKSHIRE, 1838

> Mr. Baker [an assistant inspector] proceeded, on arriving at the . . . mill . . . at once into one of the rooms (where, however, the cry of 'the Superintendent is coming' had already reached) and having observed two machines at work, with only one boy at each, but which absolutely required two, and more properly three, he cast his eye round the room, and observed some person very busy about a bag of wool; he went up and found a boy who had been wrongly employed, in the act of being concealed therein; his head and body had been already enclosed and the bag fastened over him, and Mr. Baker only discovered him by his feet still protruding . . .
>
> (*Reports of the Inspectors of Factories . . . December 1838*)

Why did the Inspectors visit without saying that they were coming? If you were a mill-owner breaking the law, how might you try to outwit them?

WOMEN FACTORY INSPECTORS

The Chief Inspector of Factories had something new to put in his Annual Report to the Home Secretary for 1893:

Factory Inspectors in Lancashire earlier this century would have been very familiar with scenes like this one, painted by L.S. Lowry in the 1930s. The mill shown, the Acme mill at Pendlebury, was built in 1905 and was the first in Lancashire to be powered by electricity. Notice its height and the many large windows.

> **Being of opinion that the field for the employment of women, within the limits of their own special capacities and aptitudes, should be as wide and as large as you could possibly make it, and that there is no field in which they could be more usefully or fruitfully employed than in looking after the health and the industrial conditions under which their fellow women labour in the factories and workshops, you appointed two ladies as inspectors, whose labours have already been found most useful ...**

One of the "useful" ladies, Miss Abrahams, suggested an improvement in her first report: read the following extract and find out what it was.

> **In the course of my visits I have found many workers ignorant of the laws which exist for their protection, and their ignorance was not solely caused by the absence of the Abstract [*a short summary of the Factory Laws*] from the workroom walls, or its effectual concealment under many orders and patterns, but from their incapacity to take in its meaning. Their first difficulty seemed to me to lie in the language, which is perhaps not sufficiently simple or brief ... the substitution of a much simpler Abstract of the law ... would lead to much greater aid being given to Her Majesty's Inspectors.**

Why, if women workers understood their rights, would they be able to give "much greater aid" to the Inspectors? What were some employers obviously doing to prevent their workers from knowing what the laws demanded?

Why do you think women inspectors were at first only allowed to inspect women workers' conditions? (Today, they do the same work as their male colleagues.)

Industrial Communities

"WITHOUT ANY ORDER OR PLAN"

You can see how an early industrial town grew up from this description, written in 1804, of Merthyr Tydvil in South Wales:

> The first houses that were built were only very small and simple cottages for furnace-men, forge-men, miners and such tradesmen as were necessary to construct the required buildings, with the common labourers who were employed to assist them. These cottages were most of them built in scattered confusion, without any order or plan. As the [iron] works increased, more cottages were wanted and erected in the spaces between those that had been previously built, till they became so connected with each other, as to form... irregular streets.... These streets are now many in number, close and confined, having no proper outlets between the houses. They are consequently very filthy for the most part, and doubtless very unhealthy. Some streets ... have within these few years been built, and more are building, on a better plan; in straighter lines, and wider, having decent houses, with commodious outlets, and other necessary attentions to cleanliness and health. In some of the early ... streets, we frequently see the small, miserable houses taken down and larger and very seemly ones built in their stead. (B.II. Malkin, *The Scenery, Antiquities and Biography of South Wales, 1804*)

In the early days of industrial development, living conditions for industrial workers were often unpleasant and unhealthy. Workers' houses were put up quickly and cheaply. Sanitation was often non-existent. Some enlightened employers tried to improve matters, but government action was needed too. Slowly, laws were passed to improve sanitation and housing. Local councils were encouraged to build decent "council houses" for working people.

LIVING NEAR OLD-STYLE INDUSTRIES

Mines and ironworks spoilt their surroundings, and little was done at first to make industrial towns and villages pleasant or healthy places in which to live. The following description is again of Merthyr and of nearby Bedwellty:

> Their houses are ranged round the works in rows.... The surface of the soil around is frequently blackened with coal, or covered with high mounds of refuse from the mines and the furnaces. The road between the rows is so imperfectly made as to be often, in wet weather, ankle deep in black mud. Flat pavement is rarely seen.... Volumes of smoke from the furnaces, the rolling mills and the coke-hearths, are driven past.... Gardens are few, and almost entirely neglected. Due attention to sewerage is also overlooked. The house of the master or resident director stands conspicuous amidst a small group of stunted and blackened trees... (*Report to the Committee of Council for Education, 1839*)

Why would the trees be "stunted and blackened"?

In 1845, the Victorian author and MP, Benjamin Disraeli, wrote a book called *Sybil: or The Two Nations* to draw the attention of one "nation", the rich, to the misery of the other "nation", the poor. (If you look in the Date List (page 45), you can see how he helped working people when he was Prime Minister (1874-80).) He invented as one of the characters in his novel a factory owner called Mr. Trafford:

When the work people of Mr. Trafford left his factory they were not forgotten ... one of his first efforts had been to build a village where every family might be well lodged [and] ... his workmen ... proud of their house and their little garden. ... In every street there was a well: behind the factory were the public baths; the schools were under the direction of the ... curate of the church, which Mr. Trafford ... had raised and endowed [*provided money for its upkeep*]. In the midst of this village, surrounded by beautiful gardens ... was the house of Trafford himself. ... The vast form of the spreading factory, the roofs and gardens of the village, the ... chimneys of the house of Trafford, the spire of the ... church, with the sparkling river and the sylvan [*wooded*] background, came ... on the sight [of the visitor] ...

A real factory owner, Titus Salt of Bradford, is said to have been influenced by this description when he founded, in 1851, a model village around his new factory in the country. He called his village "Saltaire", and you can still see it today. You can visit Bournville, too, near Birmingham. (Which firm, making which product, built that model village?)

This "Bird's Eye View of group of cottages & cesspool referred to in the report on Preston" was attached to the 1844 Report of the Commission on the State of Large Towns.

The Report itself describes how: "Between the Back Yards of the two rows of Cottages, a Cesspool extends the whole length of the Street, which receives the Contents of the Privies & Drains, & the ashes & refuse of the whole Block. ... The Contents of the Cesspool belong to the Landlord, and are taken out twice a year."

Notice the mills at the back of the cottages. Who would have lived in these rows? Does it surprise you that the average age of death for "Operatives and their families" in Preston at this time was 18.28 years? (Remember this average includes all the young babies who died.)

Transporting the Goods

Coal and iron, as you know, are heavy and bulky. So are some manufactured goods like china dishes, and these are fragile too. The average eighteenth-century road was rough and stony in dry weather and muddy when it rained. Although improvements were gradually made to the roads, many industries preferred to use the new canals, built in and after the 1760s. Then came the development of railways: by 1850, most major cities were linked by railway lines, and heavy goods could be carried quickly by steam trains. The canals slowly declined. (Now it is the railways which are losing their goods-traffic – to what other form of present-day transport?)

THE OLD SYSTEM

Till about the middle of the last [the eighteenth] century the trade of Sheffield was still confined and precarious, none of the manufacturers ventured to extend their trade beyond the limits of this island, and old persons still remember the time when all the produce of their smithies was conveyed weekly to London, on roads of a very different description to those which now exist, by a drove of pack horses.
(Edward Baines, *Baines's Yorkshire*, 1822)

Have you ever bumped across a stretch of unmade road? If so, you'll have some idea of what the "roads of a very different description to those which now exist" were like.

EARLY CANALS

James Brindley built the first important new canal for the Duke of Bridgewater. It carried coal from the Duke's mines at Worsley to Manchester. When the canal opened in 1761, the price of coal at Manchester was halved. Brindley later worked on the Grand Trunk Canal which linked the river Trent to the Mersey. Samuel Smiles described a difficult stretch on the canal:

. . . the engineering appliances of those early days were very limited . . . workmen were as yet only half-educated in the expert use of tools. The tunnel [carrying the canal through Harecastle Hill] . . . was little larger than a sewer, and admitted the passage of only one narrow boat, seven feet wide, at a time, involving very heavy labour. . . . This was performed by what was called legging. The Leggers lay upon the deck . . . and, by thrusting their feet against the slimy roof or sides of the tunnel . . . they contrived to push it through . . . after 'legging' Harecastle Tunnel which is more than a mile and a half long, the men were usually completely exhausted and as wet from perspiration as if they had been dragged through the canal itself. The process occupied about two hours . . .
(*Lives of the Engineers*, 1878)

You can see in the picture the wider tunnel Telford built to replace Brindley's narrow one.

Telford's new Harecastle Tunnel was wider than the tunnel first built by Brindley. You can see the tow-path: horses pulled the boats through. How can you tell that the tunnel is absolutely straight?

RAILWAYS BRING WORK TO DERBY

New forms of transport meant new jobs. Labourers called "navvies" laid the railway lines (some of the books listed on page 47 can help you find out about them) and there was plenty of work for skilled men, as the railway companies began to establish their own workshops.

With the opening of the railways, the prosperity of Derby became assured: iron works sprang up to supply the new means of locomotion with forgings and castings; the railway companies, finding coal and iron close at hand, established engineering works at Derby for constructing their locomotives and rolling stock, and the town began to grow at a rate never before known. (A.W. Davison, *Derby – Its Rise and Progress*, 1906)

What other jobs were and are provided by the railways?

Engines made in British railway-workshops were sent all over the world. This photograph was taken about seventy years ago. What tells you that this is a steam engine? Notice the name of the firm (Craven Bros) that made the girder near the top of the picture, and the huge size of the workshop.

MOVING COAL FROM THE COAL-FIELDS IN THE 1890s

The important question of the disposal of the produce at a colliery receives consideration before the shafts are sunk, although the exact route of the tramway or railway may not then be decided on. The necessities of small collieries may be met by a cart trade or by a neighbouring canal. Where the output is large, and especially if the coal raised is for steaming purposes [*for use in steamships*] a ship canal or a railway to carry the coal to ... a seaport, or to the staithes [*loading-places*] alongside a navigable river, becomes an absolute necessity for inland collieries. (*The Colliery Manager's Handbook, 1891*)

Notice all the different types of transport available by this date. Do you know, or can you work out, what a "ship canal" is?

More Goods to Buy

In factories, goods could be "mass-produced" – machine-made in large quantities. Workers could specialize in operating machines making just one part of an article. This made factory work boring, but by the end of the nineteenth century there were many more things that ordinary people could afford to buy.

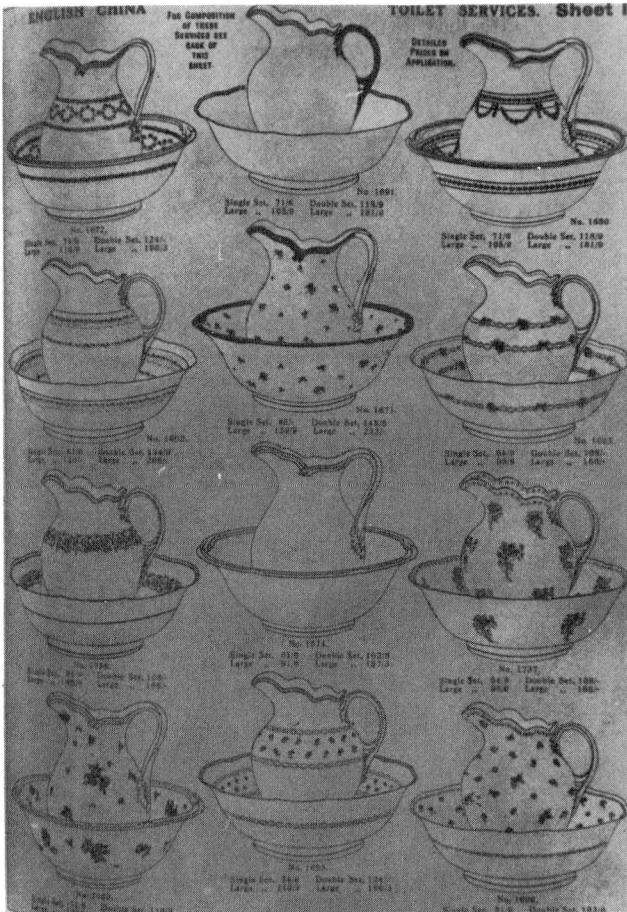

Everyone who could possibly afford to bought a washing-stand set like these. Why were they so popular in the days before most houses had bathrooms? These sets were advertised by the Army and Navy Stores in London in 1907. They are mass-produced, so they are only made to two basic patterns. Can you pick out these two shapes? What has been done to make the sets look different from each other?

The American Elihu Burritt described in 1868 the development of a Birmingham company (Gillott's) making steel pens:

> [The first steel pen] was made to resemble a quill pen in shape, and was gradually developed into a beautiful but expensive article. Some . . . were sold as high as five shillings each. . . . So late as 1839 they were almost unknown to the general public, but in the following ten years they arose to an important place among the manufactures of the town . . . the quantity made . . . amounts to over 14,000,000 of pens a week. . . . To show what improved machinery has done to cheapen and multiply their production, it may suffice to say, that pens that were sold . . . thirty years ago at five shillings a gross are now sold as low as a halfpenny per gross, or two dozen for a single farthing! The Birmingham pen-makers are beginning to encounter considerable competition in the foreign market from manufactories recently established in the United States, in France, and Germany. But there is room for all . . . (Elihu Burritt, *Walks in the Black Country*, 1868)

What cheap, mass-produced writing implement has replaced the steel pen for us today? Can you find out when it first became available in Britain, and which country first produced it?

Why did Gillott's need to move into this large factory? [

NEW MACHINES IN THE HOME

During the past ten years sewing machines have been introduced into most manufactories and workshops devoted to the production of articles of clothing, and are gradually coming to be regarded as indispensable in the equipment of a house. The sewing-machine is a decided favourite with the ladies, and mothers who have to bring up large families on limited incomes find it a 'friend indeed'. (David Bremner, *Industries of Scotland*, 1869)

An American, Isaac Singer, produced the first practical sewing-machine in 1851. By 1865, you could buy a Singer "Family" model for £4.4s.

What machines have you got in your home today?

Experiments *upon the properties of the metal used, and the various modes of construction, is now before the Public in* **GILLOTT'S NEW PATENT STEEL PEN**, *which, being constructed upon a principle perfectly new, combines all the advantages of the Elasticity and Fineness of the Quill with the Durability of the Metallic Pen, and thus obviates all the objections hitherto existing against the use of Steel Pens. The Patentee is proud in acknowledging that a discerning Public has paid the most gratifying tribute to the value of his humble, though useful labours, by a demand for the* **NEW PATENT STEEL PEN** *beyond his means of supply in the premises he lately occupied; he has therefore, now to announce that he has taken the whole of the above Premises, which will enable him to execute the increasing orders with which he has lately been favoured, with all possible accuracy and dispatch.*

Sold also Wholesale and Retail by S. Hutton at his Warehouse, No 26 High Street, Birming.

MASS-PRODUCTION IN THE FOOD INDUSTRY

David Bremner was fascinated by one Scottish firm that had taken advantage of new technology (the first experiments in tinning food were made early in the nineteenth century).

In 1837 Messrs. John Gillon & Co. established a provision preservatory in Mitchell Street, Leith. . . . The trade-list of the firm contains about 500 varieties of preserved meats, soups, vegetables, fish, game, etc. . . . In the stores hundreds of thousands of canisters painted of a uniform red are piled in bins. Each canister bears a label which, besides indicating the contents, describes the mode of preparing them for the table. . . . The prices are so low . . . that persons may obtain, in some cases, the preserved provisions at a cheaper rate than they require to pay for the same articles in an unprepared state [*fresh*]. . . . In order to make the tin canisters by the usual method, more than 100 tinsmiths would be required, but this part of the work is accomplished by machines worked by men and lads, who can learn the business perfectly in the course of a few weeks. Messrs. Gillon & Co. . . . purchased the patent for canister-making machinery from an American inventor.

As well as tinned food, what other "preserved provisions" can we now buy?

Look again at the extracts. Which other countries are competing with British industry by the 1860s and after? Is there any evidence that any of them is out-stripping Britain?

33

Trade Unions

As workers congregated in factories, mines and industrial towns, they began to band together to bargain with employers. At first, this alarmed both employers and the government and "combinations" of workers were forbidden. During the nineteenth and early twentieth centuries, however, progress was made towards the development of a strong Trade Union movement which could work for improvements in wages and conditions.

A LAW AGAINST "COMBINATION"

> Every ... workman ... who shall at any time after the passing of this Act enter into any combination to obtain an advance [*increase*] of wages, or to lessen or alter the hours or duration of the time of working, or to decrease the quantity of work ... and who shall be lawfully convicted ... shall ... be committed to ... gaol for any time not exceeding 3 calendar months ...
> (*Combination Act, 1800*)

This law remained in force until 1824.

Today, the Trade Unions need to contact workers who have come to Britain from other countries, many of them Commonwealth countries. This TUC pamphlet was first published in 1979.

Trades Union Congress

BRITISH TRADE UNIONS

AN INTRODUCTION FOR NEWCOMERS TO THIS COUNTRY

... A union bargains with employers to get better pay, better holidays and safer working conditions.

... It protects you against victimisation and seeks to get you, and your fellow workers, a fair deal.

... British trade unions are committed to oppose racial discrimination and to win equality for all groups in the community.

British trade unions already represent nearly twelve million workers in this country. Whatever job you are doing there is a union for you. For more information, see inside.

A VICTORIAN TRADE UNIONIST

John Ward of Clitheroe belonged to the Weavers' Union (the first really effective Unions were set up by skilled workers). In his diary, he describes Union activities:

> **1860 June 13. Another fine day. We had a Public meeting of weavers tonight to hear a deputy from the executive who was sent to get up an agitation in favour of the operatives of Colne who are out on strike for an advance of wages. There are about 1500 hands out so we agreed to pay twopence per loom. A committee was chosen, of which I am one.**
> **June 23 ... we sent £28 to Colne.**
> **November 17. It is a poor week, this, owing to Mercers' [mill] and part of Low Moor being broken down. We could only send £20 to Colne ...**

By February 1861, John Ward's own mill, Low Moor, was proposing to cut wages because the American Civil War was preventing cotton supplies from getting to England.

> **February 2 We are all out [on strike] at Low Moor.**
> **February 23 ... tonight we sent the last subscription to Colne for a while ...**
> **March 2 We took £100 out of the bank and gave 1/6 each to every member of the Union who was out of work ...**

(The Low Moor men agreed a smaller wage-cut in April and went back to work).

> **April 12 ... they [the employers] seem determined to get rid of every committee man ... as all blame is attached to them.**

How did the Weavers' Union help its members? What risk was there in being a committee member?

In 1867 a Royal Commission was set up to investigate Trade Unions. As you can see, employers and workers described the effects of Union activities in different ways:

> The employers complain that trades unions have fostered a spirit of antagonism between themselves and their workmen which formerly did not exist. There is no longer, they say, the cordial and friendly feeling which used to be common between the two classes. The workmen, looking rather to the approval of their Unions than to that of their employers . . . are less anxious . . . to stand well with the latter; and the employers on their part no longer feel under the same obligation to look after the interests of their workmen and to assist them in periods of difficulty. Misunderstandings . . . are exasperated and prolonged . . .
>
> To this it is replied on the part of the Unions, that their . . . tendency . . . is to raise . . . the character of the workman, by making him feel that he is . . . a member of a strong united body, capable at once of defending his rights and of ensuring him a resource in case of temporary need. It is maintained also that the practice of having a code of working rules agreed to between employers and workmen . . . embracing [*including*] a book of wages, of laws, and of trade rules . . . tends to diminish and usually extinguish the occurrence of strikes, and to establish a spirit of co-operation between masters and workmen. (*Report of the Royal Commission on Trade Unions*, 1869)

Look at the arguments of each side: do you think either side is completely right or completely wrong?

WOMEN IN THE UNIONS

Though many women worked in factories, the early Trade Unions were chiefly concerned about men's wages and most of their members were men. However, a woman trade unionist managed to win support from the 1888 Trades Union Congress for an important resolution:

> That in the opinion of this Congress it is desirable, in the interests of both man and woman, that in trades where women do the same work as men, they shall receive the same payment.

You can find out from the Date List (page 45) when equal pay for the same work was finally achieved. Efforts are still being made today to encourage more women to join unions. A slogan in 1983 was:

> A Woman's Place is in her Union

A POWERFUL ARGUMENT

In the late nineteenth and early twentieth centuries unskilled workers also formed unions. Ernest Bevin, who worked for the Dockers Union, argued in July 1914 in favour of strong amalgamated unions (which banded together a number of small unions).

> It is not so much that it means a power to attack, as a power to negotiate, and that power to negotiate is the most valuable thing that we can have. Where there is practically one Union covering all transport and the bulk of the general labourers-unions in one town, what is the first thing the employers ask? It is 'Will you all strike together?'

In 1922 Bevin's work helped to create the Transport and General Workers' Union which began with 300,000 members. Are there, do you think, any disadvantages in belonging to a very large Union?

═Nineteenth-Century Wonders═

Industrial Britain has produced many exciting and beautiful things and is still producing them today (have you seen Concorde? or the Humber Bridge? or the Thames Barrier at Woolwich?)

How do you get a canal across a river? Telford built the Pontcysyllte aqueduct (at the back of the picture) to carry the Ellesmere Canal over the river Dee. Opened in 1805, it is 127 feet high and over 1,000 feet long. The canal water is carried in an iron trough (shown in the small picture). How does the old road bridge over the river compare with the aqueduct?

Today, you can still cross the aqueduct, either on a canal holiday cruiser or by walking along the tow-path.

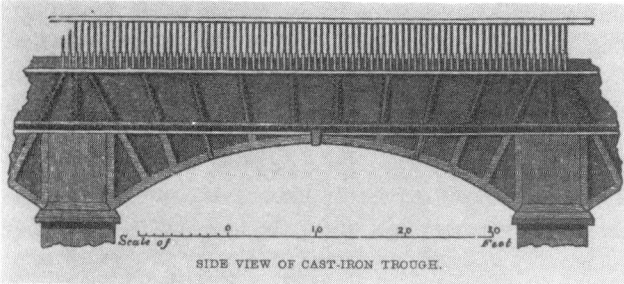

SIDE VIEW OF CAST-IRON TROUGH.

TRAINS AND TELEGRAPH

In 1832 the young Scot Alexander Somerville saw his first train. He vividly remembered the occasion when he wrote his autobiography:

> **All sights which I had seen . . . shrunk into comparative nothingness, when, after reaching Liverpool, I went into the country a week, in the neighbourhood of Prescot, and saw (each day I sought to see it, each hour of the day I could have stood to see it again) the white steam shooting through the landscape of trees, meadows and villages, and the long train, loaded with merchandise, men and women and human enterprise, rolling along under the steam. . . . In wonder alone, the electric telegraph outstrips the railway; but they belong to the one family of wonders . . .**
> (*Autobiography of a Working Man*, 1848)

What would you include in a "family of wonders" for today?

The great engineer Isambard Kingdom Brunel began his career building bridges and railways, but he also designed ships. Though paddle steamers had been used for short trips from 1812, it was not until the 1830s that such steamers crossed the Atlantic. The chief problem, as Brunel later explained, was

> making the vessel *large enough to carry its own coal* . . . when the 'Great Western' was projected for the New York line, the passage had been considered an impossible one for steamboats. . . . Certainly, no steamboat then built could get across except by a chance fair weather passage, and then only by being completely filled with coals and leaving no room for passengers or cargo. Simply by building a ship of the size necessary to take the coal, over and above the accommodation required for a due number of passengers and a reasonable quantity of cargo, the passage was rendered perfectly easy and certain . . .
>
> The increased size, instead of being a disadvantage, was found . . . to be a great benefit, and gave increased speed . . . (*Letter to Directors of Eastern Steam Company* 10 June, 1852)

The *Great Western's* first sailing from Bristol to New York was advertised in 1838:

STEAM TO NEW YORK
The
Great Western
of 1340 Tons Register,
and 450 Horse Power
Strongly built, Coppered and Copper-fastened, with Engines of the very best construction, by Maudslay, Sons and Field, AND EXPRESSLY ADAPTED FOR THE BRISTOL AND NEW YORK STATION
Lieut. JAMES HOSKEN, R.N., Commander,
Will sail DIRECT from Bristol On the 7th April 1838 AT TWO O'CLOCK IN THE AFTERNOON
The rate of Cabin Passage is 35 guineas . . .
This ship has coal storage for 25 Days' constant steaming, and therefore will not require to touch at Cork for Coal.

What information about the ship does this advertisement give us?

In the end, the *Great Western* sailed on 8 April. She arrived at New York on 23 April, a few hours after a smaller steamship, *Sirius*. However, *Sirius* had used up all her coal (taken on at Cork in Ireland), while the *Great Western* had plenty left.

One of Brunel's ships, the *Great Britain*, has been restored and is now on show in Bristol.

A NEW SIGHT IN LONDON

The latest and the most striking of all the London Bridges is the Tower Bridge. This bridge is designed on the bascule principle, with two arms which, dividing in the middle, can be raised by means of weights . . . in order to allow the passage of ships. . . . The great bascule can be lifted in a minute and a half. The rapid elevation of these gigantic arms and the passage of a ship through the bridge is one of the most striking sights of London. On Saturday, June 30, 1894, the bridge was formally opened by the Prince of Wales . . . (*London South of the Thames*, Walter Besant, 1912)

What is so special about Tower Bridge? Why is it not often raised today?

Industrial Exhibitions

Prince Albert, Queen Victoria's husband, started a fashion when he organized a "Great Exhibition of the Works of all Nations" in 1851, to demonstrate Britain's industrial progress. There followed an exhibition in New York in 1853 and the first of a series of Paris Exhibitions in 1855. You may be able to find souvenirs from such International Exhibitions in museums. Some of the objects which were displayed have survived too: there is a huge block of coal (weighing 15 tons) in Bedwellty Park, Tredegar, Gwent, which was originally cut for display in the 1851 Exhibition.

QUEEN VICTORIA ENJOYS THE GREAT EXHIBITION

The Queen opened the Exhibition in its special glass building, the Crystal Palace in Hyde Park, on 1 May 1851. She then made more visits to see different sections of the display, recording her impressions in her Journal.

> **May 29** ... to the Exhibition ... we examined ... all the textiles.
>
> **June 7** To the Exhibition: went to the machinery part, where we remained 2 hours, and which is excessively interesting and instructive, and fills one with admiration for the greatness of man's mind, which can devise and carry out such wonderful inventions, contributing to the welfare and comfort of the whole world ...

> **July 9** We went to the Exhibition and had the electric telegraph show explained and demonstrated before us. It is the most wonderful thing, and the boy who works it does so with the greatest ease and rapidity.

The 1851 Exhibition had over 6 million visitors and made a large profit (£186, 437, enough to buy land at South Kensington on which to build museums, including the Science Museum). Do you know what happened to the "Crystal Palace"?

A hundred years later, another exhibition (but a smaller, national one) was held in London – the Festival of Britain. Do you know or can you find out which important building (still in use) was built for that exhibition?

USED ALL OVER THE WORLD.

Chili, 1875.
Brussels, 1876.
Cape Town, 1877.
Paris, 1878.
Torino, 1879.
London, 1883.
International Fisheries,
Sweden, 1883.

Glasgow, 1885.
Port Elizabeth, 1885.
Liverpool, 1886.
Adelaide, 1887.
Barcelona, 1888.
Sydney, 1888.
Melbourne, 1889.
Dunedin, 1890.

JOHN SHAW, SHEFFIELD, ENGLAND.

SPECIAL IMPROVED

Steel Wire Ropes

OF THE FINEST QUALITY, FOR

MINING, PLOUGH ROPES, INCLINES, SHIPS' HAWSERS, CABLES, TRAWL WARPS, HOISTING GEAR, &c.

Wire all carefully tested and quality guaranteed.

SPECIAL STEEL WOVE WORK for Gold Dressing.

Copper Rope Lightning Conductors, Sash Cords, Gilt & Silver Picture Cord, &c.

PATENT LOCK WEDGE AND ALL KINDS OF FENCING.

You can make a list of countries holding exhibitions between 1875 and 1890 from this Sheffield firm's advertisement (use your atlas to find unfamiliar towns, and remember we call "Torino" "Turin"). What were the wire ropes used for, and why are they better than ordinary ropes for some jobs?

THE BRITISH EMPIRE EXHIBITION, 1924

You can find out from the following advertisement why Britain put on this exhibition (remember that by 1924 Britain was no longer the leading industrial country). What was being done to make the exhibition attractive to visitors?

THE GATEWAY TO THE WORLD

You must not miss the glories of Wembley.

Mankind throughout the centuries has never known a spectacle so wonderful. You will wander at your will in the magnificent Palaces of Industry and Engineering. Towers and pinnacles, domes and minarets, proclaim the range and splendour of our Commonwealth of Nations.

Designed to delight the eye, the British Empire Exhibition has a definite national purpose – to demonstrate to the ends of the earth what British skill and enterprise can achieve.

At Wembley the trader will increase his trade, the student his knowledge, the holidaymaker his pleasure.

The spacious Stadium, the music, the illuminated lakes, the glorious gardens, the broad highways, the Amusement Park of a thousand thrills – these are but a tithe [*a tenth*] of the triumphs that make Wembley the event of a lifetime.

Admission 1/6d
Children 9d

H.M. THE KING WILL PROCLAIM THE GATE – WIDE OPEN
at Wembley
on April 23rd.

(*Bromley and District Times*, 18 April 1924)

What do we use the "spacious stadium" for today?

This postcard shows the elaborate buildings planned ▷ for the Scottish National Exhibition of 1908. Read the message. What other exhibition was opening in Britain in that year? and where? (The address gives the clue).

A TRADER HOPES TO "INCREASE HIS TRADE" THROUGH THE 1924 EXHIBITION

EASTMAN'S
the London Dyers & Cleaners
for over one hundred and
twenty years, are devoting this
space to advertise the
**BRITISH EMPIRE
EXHIBITION**
Wembley, April to September
The Wonderful Exhibits of
BRITISH DYEING & CLEANING
shown by Eastman's will prove
well worth your inspection.
Call at STAND NO. H277
MISCELLANEOUS TEXTILE SECTION
and obtain free of charge an
Illustrated Guide to London.
EASTMAN & SON (Dyers & Cleaners) Ltd.
(*Bromley and District Times*, 1924)

Today, few large general International Exhibitions are held (they are very expensive and difficult to organize). Industries have their own Fairs or Shows, though – have you been to any or seen any advertised?

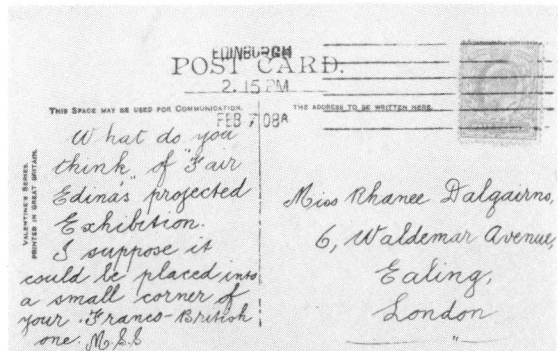

Scottish National Exhibition, Edinburgh, 1908

Preserving the Past

Great efforts are being made today to preserve old industrial buildings and machinery. Sometimes whole areas are preserved – turned into open-air industrial museums like the one at Ironbridge in Shropshire, or converted for new purposes like St Katharine's Dock in London with its marina, old-ship collection and shops and restaurants for tourists. Many industrial landmarks have already been lost, however. You will find that people have different views on what is worth preserving and on how much money can be spared to preserve it.

Today, a visit to an old industrial site makes a popular outing.

MINING MUSEUMS

RHONDDA TO REMEMBER PIT PAST AT A MUSEUM

A mining museum is to be created at a former colliery in the Rhondda Valley....

As grass returns to parts of the Rhondda that have been blackened for a century, the campaign by local people to establish the museum has been spurred by the colliery closure programme... councillors are planning to use the Lewis Merthyr colliery site where mining ceased earlier this year, as the museum headquarters....

The Mayor of Rhondda ... said ... "This museum ... will celebrate our heritage. It will also ... bring people in and provide jobs in the tourist and service industries".
(*The Guardian*, 17 October 1983)

Why are people in the Rhondda Valley supporting the idea of a mining-museum there?

Other areas have already converted old coal mines into museums: you can see pictures of one of these on page 12 and page 21. There is another at Chatterley Whitfield in Staffordshire.

INDUSTRIAL MUSEUMS

The Sheffield Industrial Museum was first opened to the public on 1 May 1982. Since then, 5,000 visitors a month have seen its exhibits. Peter Smithurst [keeper of the Museum]... likes to think of the museum as 'a tribute to the people of Sheffield past and present who worked and still work in industry' ... (*Radio Times*, July 1983)

INDUSTRIAL WORKERS' EXPERIENCES

One other way of preserving the past it to record people's memories of their working life. Sometimes this is done for radio or TV programmes. In 1983, Channel Four made video-tapes of interviews with car-workers at British Leyland's Cowley works at Oxford, and used these for a series on the history of the motor industry. The following extract comes from a book of written accounts of their work by various people.

The author of this particular account, Patrick McGeown, was a steelmaker and here he explains why he liked his job:

> There was drama in it, in the flowing steel, and in the noise, and in the blast furnaces away to the right where the hot iron was filling in the sand beds. Drama too in the nearby rolling mill where the strips of steel became longer and longer and faded slowly from a white glow to a dull red. . . . I don't think that I was more than a week in that place before I knew that I would never leave steel. . . . There were things that I hated, and the night work was one of them, but nothing drove me away . . .
> (*Work 2*, ed. Ronald Fraser, Pelican Original, 1969)

You could make your own collection of people's memories of their work, either on tape, if you own or can borrow a tape-recorder, or on paper.

You may have seen some of the TV programmes about museums short-listed each year for the "Museum of the Year" award. The Sheffield Industrial Museum was short-listed in 1983, and the Gladstone Pottery Museum won the award in 1976. You will find more industrial museums in the list of Places to Visit on pages 45-46.

These bottle-ovens or kilns are preserved in the Gladstone Pottery Museum. They were used to bake china and earthenware: can you see what fuel heated them? In 1939 there were 2,300 bottle ovens in Stoke-on-Trent, helping to give the town its nickname "Smoky Stoke". Today's kilns are fired by gas, oil or electricity, and bottle-ovens and smoke have gone.

WORKING FOR PRESERVATION

> An army of volunteers, with a roll-call totalling to hundreds, toiled to clean up the site [of the Gladstone Pottery, Longton] and then to make the buildings and machinery ready for visitors. The members of the trust that had been set up for the purpose created committees and working parties to raise funds . . . (*Guide to the Gladstone Pottery Museum*)

This extract shows two important ways in which people can help to preserve the industrial past. What are they? Can you think of any other ways of helping?

Britain is again going through a period of industrial change, but today she is in competition with many other industrial countries.

TWO FACES OF BRITISH INDUSTRY IN THE 1980s

A description of Consett, County Durham

The town itself seems unremarkable until you reach its heart and go past the Job Centre to a complex of tall coke ovens, gasometers, cooling towers, and blast furnaces. All is silent and deserted, and in large measure ruined: factories are open to the sky through steel-skeleton roofs. . . . It all looks as if it had recently been bombed. . . . Solid brown rows of thirties stone houses [*i.e. houses built in the 1930s*] stand back from the deserted works; one or two middle-aged men emerge in the early afternoon sunlight to walk their dogs . . . (*David Gentleman's Britain*, Weidenfeld and Nicolson, 1982)

A new factory at Newport, Gwent

At first sight [Richard] Rogers's *Inmos* building looks like a beached space station. . . . Gleaming silver and blue, it sits on a cushion of lush Welsh meadow. . . . The space [idea] is given extra force by the fact that this is Britain's first full-blown silicon chip factory, in which the workforce has to don astronaut-type protective clothing and visors before moving into the production areas through carefully protected airlocks . . . (*The Sunday Times*, 17 April 1983)

What has happened to Consett's steelworks? What is being made at Newport's new factory?

MODERN COAL MINES

The Selby coalfield, the largest in Europe, went into production yesterday . . .

Coal runs on a giant underground conveyor belt and is eventually brought to the surface at a huge development called the Gascoigne Wood drift mine, reminiscent of [*like*] a futuristic railway station. It is then loaded on trains and taken directly to local power stations for burning. . . . The whole development has blended in so well that the local residents are no longer complaining about the development . . . (*The Guardian,* 5 July 1983)

Mr. Ian MacGregor, newly installed Chairman of the National Coal Board, crawled on his hands and knees along a coalface yesterday six miles out under the North Sea. . . . After two and a half hours underground at Wearmouth Colliery in Sunderland, riding underground trains, and talking to miners, he emerged. . . . Wearmouth Colliery is certainly not threatened with closure. The mine, although one of the oldest in the country, has enormous reserves. . . . Most of the output is shipped to the Tameside power station. . . . Before he left, Mr. MacGregor, aged 71, brushed off any suggestions that the trip had been strenuous. He had to walk a mile underground before he made his journey on hands and knees to the coalface. Crawling about was the only way to work on a 42 inch seam he said. (*The Guardian,* 10 September 1983)

Compare these reports with accounts of coal-mining earlier in this book. What changes do you notice? What has not changed?

What is most of the coal produced by these particular mines being used for? Why does the second report stress that "Wearmouth Colliery is . . . not threatened with closure"?

Notice that Mr MacGregor is Chairman of the National Coal Board. Do you know, or can you find out, when coal was nationalized?

UNEMPLOYMENT

There are more than 3 million people unemployed in Britain in 1984. There are many arguments over the reasons for this (you might like to collect newspaper cuttings which put different points of view). The figures below show job-losses in just two old-established British industries between 1977 and 1981.

Employees in employment (Great Britain and Northern Ireland)

	1977	1978	1979	1980	1981
Iron and steel (general)	239,000	215,000	206,000	180,000	138,000
Textiles	512,000	490,000	478,000	424,000	363,000

(*Annual Abstract of Statistics*, 1983 Edition)

Look again at the first extract: where is one place where steel workers have lost jobs?

NEW INDUSTRY IN SCOTLAND

Some areas of Britain have been greatly affected by the discovery of oil in the North Sea. One of these is Shetland, where Jo Grimond, now Lord Grimond, was MP from 1950 to 1983.

. . . the impact of the terminal [on Sullom Voe] is heavy. . . . It is during the construction period that a great number of workers is needed. . . . By 1978 . . . four thousand were employed, over three thousand of whom were incomers living in completely self-contained camps . . a [Shetland] girl who had been earning £40 a week in a shop in 1977 found herself a job at £90 making beds, with free transport and meals thrown in . . .

Lerwick Harbour is full of strange vessels such as ocean-going tugs and oil-platform supply vessels with their high bridges fore and their low platforms astern. Sometimes when you look across the harbour from Lerwick a tall rig illuminated at night like a Christmas tree lies, an exotic monster. . . . Lerwick harbour now extends some two miles from its old confines. . . . Sumburgh airport, which when I first arrived there was a single hut, now hums all day with aeroplanes and helicopters. (Jo Grimond, *Memoirs*, 1979)

What changes did the establishment of the oil-terminal bring to Shetland? Do you think they were for the better? or the worse?

Difficult Words

bascule	This French word for "see-saw" describes something balanced so that one end moves up when a weight is put on the other end (and down when the weight is removed).
bobbin	wooden pin on which thread is wound.
card-room hands	workers in the card-room of a textile mill, where wool, etc, was "combed" with an iron-toothed instrument.
company shop	shop owned by the firm, where workers were compelled or "expected" to buy provisions, often using vouchers given to them instead of money wages.
dressers (of cloth)	workers who smoothed and trimmed the cloth.
engine-wright	the man who worked an engine.
kitchen-range	a fire-grate with ovens attached.
mass-production	making objects in large numbers (often by dividing an object up into sections, with each group of workers producing just one section).
molten	melted.
noxious	harmful, destructive.
pack-horses	horses carrying goods in bags or baskets slung on their backs.
piecers	children who pieced together (i.e. mended) broken threads.
pigs (of iron)	lumps or slabs of iron made by pouring molten iron into rough moulds or channels made in sand.
reelers	workers on the machines that wound the thread.
rolling mills	places where metal was rolled out by machinery into sheets, bars, etc.
Royal Commission	a group of people appointed by the King or Queen, on the advice of the Prime Minister, to investigate and report on a particular problem.
smelt	heat ore to extract metal.
truck or tommy	wages paid in goods instead of money. "Truck Acts" from the eighteenth century onwards forbade this, but the laws were disobeyed.
twisters-in	workers who twist the threads of a new warp to join one already woven, to make a long piece of cloth.
warpers	workers who prepare the warp (the set of threads stretched lengthwise on a loom) for the weavers.

CONVERSION TABLE

NEW MONEY		OLD MONEY
1p	=	2.4d
5p	=	1s. (1 shilling)
50p	=	10s. (10 shillings)
£1	=	£1
		12d = 1 shilling
		20 shillings = £1
£1.05	=	21 shillings (a guinea)

Date List

(Reform of working and living conditions)

1802   Health and Morals of Apprentices Act – the first "Factory" Act, which tried, unsuccessfully, to protect poor children sent to work in textile mills.

1833   Factory Act – no children under 9 to work in textile mills; children 9-13 not to work more than 9 hours a day; children 13-18 not more than 12 hours a day. Four Factory Inspectors appointed.

1837 Births had to be registered, so it became easier to find out how old a child was.

1842 Mines Act – women, and children under 10, forbidden to work underground.

1844 Factory Act – a 6½-hour day for children under 13 in textile factories (but they could start work at 8 years of age). Machinery had to be fenced.

1847 Ten Hour Act – women and everyone under 18 not to work more than 10 hours a day in textile factories.

1850 Inspection of Coal Mines Act – Inspectors of Mines appointed.

1864 & 1867 Factory Acts – extended factory laws and inspection to non-textile factories.

1866 Public Health Act – local authorities had to provide sewers, etc, and appoint sanitary inspectors.

1867 Workshop Act – extended factory laws to some small workshops. Forbade the employment anywhere of children under 8.

1868 Artisans' and Labourers' Dwellings Act – allowed councils to demolish unhealthy houses (but compensated the owners).

1874 Factory Act – forbade the employment of children under 10.

1875 Artisans' Dwellings Act – councils given powers to demolish whole slum areas.

1875 Public Health Act – drew together earlier health laws, set out duties of local authorities and set standards for sanitation in new housing.

1878 Factory Act – made all the factory laws clear and up-to-date.

1880 Employers had to pay compensation to workpeople injured in accidents.

1890 Housing of the Working Classes Act – local authorities were allowed to build houses themselves.

1909 Trade Boards Act – protected workers in "sweatshops" (very small workshops).

1911 Insurance against sickness, and against unemployment for some workers.

1919 Housing and Town Planning Act – the new Ministry of Health was allowed to give money for local authority house-building.

1920 Insurance against unemployment extended to most workers.

1946 National Health Service established.

1954 Mines and Quarries Act – no one under 16 to work underground.

1956 Clean Air Act – factories (and private houses too) had to reduce smoke.

1970 Equal Pay Act – women to have the same pay as men for "like" work.

1974 Health and Safety at Work Act – protects workers in all kinds of workplaces.

NB It is worth remembering that from 1867 onwards, more and more working people gained the right to vote for members of the House of Commons.

Places to Visit

NB Museum opening times vary; so do admission charges, where these are made. Check with the museum before your visit.

Armley Mill Industrial Museum, Leeds (groups from schools can work in Victorian schoolroom).

Beamish North of England Open Air Museum, Stanley, County Durham (railway and coal-mining relics, miners' cottages).

Big Pit Mining Museum, Blaenavon, Gwent (coal-mine: underground visits).

Bolton, Lancs: Steam-engine displayed in shopping centre, Deansgate.
Tonge Moor Textile Museum, Tonge Moor Road (textile machines).

Burnley Canal Toll House and Weavers' Triangle, Burnley, Lancs (textile displays and well-preserved Victorian industrial area).

Cornish Engines, East Pool Mine, Pool, Camborne, Cornwall (steam engines).

Cromford, Derbyshire: Arkwright's mill and workers' cottages.

Ellesmere Port Boat Museum, Ellesmere Port, South Wirral, Cheshire (canal boats).

Gladstone Pottery Museum, Longton, Stoke-on-Trent, Staffs (bottle-ovens, Potting-shop, etc).

Glasgow People's Palace Museum (Trade Union banners, working people's homes, etc).

Ironbridge Gorge Museum, Ironbridge, Shropshire (machinery, old coal and iron workings, the Iron Bridge).

Killhope Wheel, Weardale, County Durham (huge waterwheel, used for lead crushing).

Llechwedd Slate Caverns, Gwynedd (descent into slate-mine).

National Museum of Labour History, Limehouse Town Hall, Commercial Road, London E1.

New Lanark, Strathclyde, Scotland (millworkers' model village).

Quarry Bank Mill, Styal, Cheshire (water-powered cotton mill).

Saltaire, near Bradford, Yorkshire (model village and mill).

Science Museum, South Kensington, London (machinery, steel-making display, gas-industry display, etc)

Sheffield Industrial Museum (Bessemer Converter, working steam engine etc; also, in South Sheffield, Abbeydale Industrial Hamlet – waterwheels, cottages, etc).

Tower Bridge, London (admission price includes visit to museum to see the machinery).

Ulster Museum, Belfast (working machinery).

Welsh Miners Museum, Afan Argoed Country Park, Cynonville, Port Talbot, West Glamorgan (coal-mining and miners' family life).

This short list concentrates on a few particularly interesting places. Nowadays, local Tourist Boards produce good leaflets with information on industrial relics in their areas. The Wales Tourist Board publishes an excellent booklet describing practically every industrial site, museum, etc, in Wales (see the Book List for details). The London Tourist Board has produced *Canal Walks,* a splendid (free) guide to London's canals, with many references to local industries.

At the *Television History Centre,* 42, Queen Square, London WC1N 3AJ, they have sound and video recordings of contributions to Channel 4's series on industry. Write to the Centre for information sheets etc, and for a free booklet, *Making History, The Factory* – send a large, stamped envelope.

Book List

Books for Younger Readers

Davies, Penny, *Growing Up During the Industrial Revolution,* Batsford

Gagg, John, *Observer's Book of Canals,* Warne, 1982

Harris, Sarah, *Finding Out About Railways,* Batsford, 1982

Harris, Sarah, *Women At Work,* Batsford, 1981

Hennessey, R.A.S., *Factories,* Batsford

Hope-Simpson, Jacynth, *The Making of the Machine Age,* Heinemann, 1978

Lewis, Brenda Ralph, *Steam Engines,* Wayland, 1978

Longmans *Focus on History* series, especially *The Factory Age*

Longmans *Then and There* series, especially *The Industrial Revolution-Textiles* and *Coal, Iron and Steel*

Rawcliffe, Michael, *Finding Out About Victorian Towns,* Batsford, 1982

Sherwood, Martin, *Industry,* Franklin Watts, 1982

Thompson, Hugh, *Engineers and Engineering,* Batsford, 1976

Books for Older Readers

Batsford *Guides to the Industrial Archaeology of the British Isles*

Beckett, Derrick, *Brunel's Britain,* David & Charles, 1980

Bremner, David, *The Industries of Scotland,* 1869, re-printed David & Charles, 1968

Briggs, Asa, *Iron Bridge to Crystal Palace,* Thames & Hudson, 1979

Briggs, Asa, *Victorian Cities,* Odhams Press, 1963, Penguin, 1968

Burnett, John, *A History of the Cost of Living,* Penguin, 1969

Burritt, Elihu, *Walks in the Black Country,* 1868, re-printed Roundwood Press, 1976

Cobbett, William, *Rural Rides,* 1830, re-printed Penguin, 1967

Coleman, Terry, *The Railway Navvies,* Hutchinson, 1965, Penguin, 1968

Darley, Gillian, *Villages of Vision,* Paladin, 1978

English Historical Documents series, vols. xi and xii (parts 1 and 2)

Guest, Lady Charlotte, *Extracts from her Journal,* ed. Bessborough, John Murray, 1950

Hudson, Kenneth, *Exploring our Industrial Past,* Hodder & Stoughton, 1975

Huggett, Frank E., *Factory Life and Work,* Harrap, 1973

McCutcheon, Alan, *Wheel and Spindle – aspects of Irish Industrial History,* Blackstaff press, 1977

Pike, E. Royston, *Human Documents series,* especially *Human Documents of the Industrial Revolution,* Allen & Unwin, 1966

Rolt, L.T.C., *Victorian Engineering,* Penguin, 1970

Shaw, C. (An Old Potter), *When I was a Child,* Methuen 1903, re-printed S.R. Publishers, 1969

Shire Albums – The Potteries, Cotton Industry, etc, Shire Publications

Smiles, Samuel, *Industrial Biography,* 1863, re-printed David & Charles, 1967

Smiles, Samuel, *Lives of the Engineers,* 1862 onwards, re-printed David & Charles, 1968

Thompson, E.P., *The Making of the English Working Class,* Gollancz, 1963

Trinder, Barrie, *The Making of the Industrial Landscape,* Dent, 1982

Winter, John, *Industrial Architecture,* Studio Vista, 1970

Useful Packs, Booklets, etc

Arkwright Society, Tawney House, Matlock, Derbyshire: good documents pack (*Find Out About the Past – Sir Richard Arkwright*) and sets of slides of Derbyshire mills.

Big Pit Mining Museum, Blaenavon, Gwent: a well-illustrated Guide, and work-packs for schools.

Birmingham Canal Navigation Society (Secretary, Brades, Lower Penkridge Road, Acton Trussell, Staffs). *The BCN in Pictures* – splendid photographs of old and present-day canal scenes.

Gladstone Pottery Museum, Uttoxeter Road, Longton, Stoke-on-Trent: Guide (only 35p in 1983) packed with information on the Potteries, well-illustrated.

Lincolnshire Educational Aids Project, Bishop Grosseteste College, Lincoln LN1 3DY: *Lincoln's Waterways, Trail One* – a model of its kind, full of ideas you might use to make your own Trail, and only 75p (1983)

National Museum of Wales, Cathays Park, Cardiff: booklets on Welsh coal and iron industries.

Science Museum, South Kensington, London: quiz guides to displays, e.g. *Track Down early Railways,* a good range of cards, booklets, etc.

Wales – A Glimpse of the Past – a tourist's guide to industrial Wales published by Wales Tourist Board, 3, Castle Street, Cardiff; only 50p in 1983 and worth it for the illustrations alone.

Welsh Miners Museum, Afan Argoed Country Park, Cynonville, Port Talbot, West Glamorgan: Illustrated Guide with much general information on coal-mining and good pictures.

NB *Film-strips* – Longmans produce an excellent *Industrial Revolution* set in connection with their *Then and There* series.

Index